HIGH INCOME SKILLS IN 2023
A quick view of skills that can make you rich in 2023

Dan Gray

Copyright

All rights reserved. No part of this publication may be reproduced, distributed, or transmitted in any form or by any means, including photocopying, recording, or other electronic or mechanical methods, without the prior written permission of the publisher, except in the case of brief quotations embodied in critical reviews and certain other noncommercial uses permitted by copyright law.

Copyright © Dan Gray, 2023.

Table of content

Chapter 1
Chapter 2
Chapter 3
Chapter 4
Chapter 5
Chapter 6
Chapter 7
Chapter 8
Chapter 9
Chapter 10
Chapter 11
Chapter 12
Chapter 13

Chapter 1

Freelancing

Freelancing is a rising trend in the world of work, as more and more individuals are seeking flexible employment arrangements that will enable them to work on their own terms.

Freelancing means working independently on a project-by-project basis for numerous customers. It gives freedom, the possibility for increased profits, and the ability to construct a broad portfolio. Nevertheless, it also needs self-discipline and a desire to overcome the hurdles that come with working alone. It includes Freelance writing, Web development, graphic design and much more!

Freelance writing

Freelance writing is a sort of freelancing that includes creating material for customers on a project-by-project basis. This may involve creating articles, blog entries, marketing copy, product descriptions, and more. Freelance writers may work for a range of customers, including corporations, media outlets, and individuals.

One of the benefits of freelance writing is that it enables authors to work on a broad variety of themes and projects. Freelance writers may pick the projects they wish to work on, which enables them to concentrate on subjects they are

Table of content

Chapter 1
Chapter 2
Chapter 3
Chapter 4
Chapter 5
Chapter 6
Chapter 7
Chapter 8
Chapter 9
Chapter 10
Chapter 11
Chapter 12
Chapter 13

Chapter 1

Freelancing

Freelancing is a rising trend in the world of work, as more and more individuals are seeking flexible employment arrangements that will enable them to work on their own terms.

Freelancing means working independently on a project-by-project basis for numerous customers. It gives freedom, the possibility for increased profits, and the ability to construct a broad portfolio. Nevertheless, it also needs self-discipline and a desire to overcome the hurdles that come with working alone. It includes Freelance writing, Web development, graphic design and much more!

Freelance writing

Freelance writing is a sort of freelancing that includes creating material for customers on a project-by-project basis. This may involve creating articles, blog entries, marketing copy, product descriptions, and more. Freelance writers may work for a range of customers, including corporations, media outlets, and individuals.

One of the benefits of freelance writing is that it enables authors to work on a broad variety of themes and projects. Freelance writers may pick the projects they wish to work on, which enables them to concentrate on subjects they are passionate about or have experience in. This may lead to a more satisfying and rewarding job.

Freelance writing also provides freedom in terms of timing and location. Writers may work from home or anyplace else with an internet connection, and they can typically determine their own schedules. This might be especially tempting to people who prioritize work-life balance or who have other responsibilities.

But, freelance writing may also be a very competitive sector, and it can be tough to get steady employment. Freelance writers must be self-motivated and disciplined in order to manage their workload and fulfill their customers' deadlines. They must also be okay with uncertainty, since work may not always be constant, and there may be periods of time when they do not have any projects set up.

In order to be successful as a freelance writer, it is vital to have great writing abilities, the capacity to study and grasp a range of themes, and the ability to fulfill tight deadlines. It is also vital to have solid communication skills and the capacity to operate independently.

Ultimately, freelance writing may be a satisfying and enjoyable job for individuals who have a love for writing and are ready to put in the time and effort necessary to be successful. It provides flexibility, the ability to work on a range of projects, and the possibility to create a successful career as a writer.

Web development

Web development is a widely sought-after freelancing profession, since it provides the possibility for high pay and the chance to work on a broad variety of projects. Freelance web developers operate individually and are employed by customers to construct and manage websites.

As a freelance web developer, it is vital to have a thorough grasp of programming languages and web development tools, including HTML, CSS, JavaScript, and CMS systems such as WordPress and Drupal. It is also vital to have a thorough grasp of web design and user experience (UX) concepts, as well as the ability to work collaboratively with clients and other members of a team.

One of the benefits of freelancing web development is that it allows freedom in terms of timing and location. Freelance web developers may work from home or anyplace else with an internet connection, and they can typically create their own schedules. This might be especially tempting to people who prioritize work-life balance or who have other responsibilities.

Nevertheless, freelance web development may also be a very competitive sector, and it can be tough to secure steady employment. Freelancers must be self-motivated and disciplined in order to manage their workload and fulfill their customers' deadlines. They must also be okay with uncertainty, since work may not always be constant, and there may be periods of time when they do not have any projects set up.

Ultimately, freelancing web development may be a lucrative and enjoyable job for people who have a love for technology and are ready to put in the time and effort necessary to be successful. It provides freedom, the ability to work on a range of projects, and the possibility to establish a successful career as a web developer.

Graphic design

Graphic design is a common freelancing talent, which involves developing visual material for customers on a project-by-project basis. Graphic designers work on many projects, from logos and branding to advertising campaigns, website designs, and social media graphics.

As a freelance graphic designer, it is necessary to have a good eye for design, grasp of design concepts, color theory, typography, and layout, as well as the ability to utilize professional design tools such as Adobe Photoshop, Illustrator, and InDesign.

One big benefit of freelance graphic design is that it gives flexibility in terms of timing and location, enabling designers to work from wherever they choose with an internet connection, and perhaps determine their own timetables, which is excellent for individuals searching for work-life balance.

Yet, freelance graphic design may be a very competitive sector, and it can be tough to get steady employment. Freelancers must have great communication skills to establish good relationships with customers, set reasonable expectations, and fulfill deadlines.

Freelance graphic design may be a satisfying job for people enthusiastic about design, with the ability to work on varied projects and develop a successful career. Freelancers must be self-motivated and disciplined to thrive in the profession, as well as have good design abilities and the capacity to remain up-to-date with the newest trends and technologies.

Chapter 2

Digital marketing

Digital marketing refers to advertising and promoting items or services utilizing digital channels such as search engines, social media, email, and websites. It entails employing numerous strategies to attract and engage target audiences, create brand recognition, and generate leads or sales.

Some of the primary elements of digital marketing include search engine optimization (SEO), pay-per-click (PPC) advertising, social media marketing, email marketing, and content marketing. Digital marketers commonly engage with data analytics and insights to analyze the efficacy of their efforts and make data-driven choices.

Digital marketing is a widely sought-after freelancing expertise, since it provides freedom and the possibility for significant pay. Freelance digital marketers may work from anywhere with an internet connection and typically have the freedom to determine their own schedules. But, like any freelancing ability, it can also be very competitive, and freelancers must be self-motivated and disciplined to thrive.

Ultimately, digital marketing is an essential skill for firms wanting to reach and engage their target customers in the digital age. As a freelancing talent, it provides the opportunity for a successful and meaningful career for individuals who are enthusiastic about marketing and are ready to put in the time and effort necessary to succeed.

Social media marketing

Social media marketing is a sort of digital marketing that includes promoting a brand, product, or service via numerous social media platforms. With the advent of social media sites like Facebook, Instagram, Twitter, and LinkedIn, social media marketing has become a key element of any marketing plan.

One of the primary advantages of social media marketing is the opportunity to reach a broad and diversified audience. By generating and distributing compelling content on social media, companies may attract new consumers and establish connections with current ones. Social media platforms also allow for customized advertising, which may help firms reach certain groups and increase the success of their marketing efforts.

To establish a successful social media marketing strategy, it's vital to first identify your objectives and target audience. From there, you may design a content plan that includes a mix of various forms of material, such as photographs, videos, blog entries, and infographics. It's also crucial to

Chapter 2
Digital marketing

Digital marketing refers to advertising and promoting items or services utilizing digital channels such as search engines, social media, email, and websites. It entails employing numerous strategies to attract and engage target audiences, create brand recognition, and generate leads or sales.

Some of the primary elements of digital marketing include search engine optimization (SEO), pay-per-click (PPC) advertising, social media marketing, email marketing, and content marketing. Digital marketers commonly engage with data analytics and insights to analyze the efficacy of their efforts and make data-driven choices.

Digital marketing is a widely sought-after freelancing expertise, since it provides freedom and the possibility for significant pay. Freelance digital marketers may work from anywhere with an internet connection and typically have the freedom to determine their own schedules. But, like any freelancing ability, it can also be very competitive, and freelancers must be self-motivated and disciplined to thrive.

Ultimately, digital marketing is an essential skill for firms wanting to reach and engage their target customers in the digital age. As a freelancing talent, it provides the opportunity for a successful and meaningful career for individuals who are enthusiastic about marketing and are ready to put in the time and effort necessary to succeed.

Social media marketing

Social media marketing is a sort of digital marketing that includes promoting a brand, product, or service via numerous social media platforms. With the advent of social media sites like Facebook, Instagram, Twitter, and LinkedIn, social media marketing has become a key element of any marketing plan.

One of the primary advantages of social media marketing is the opportunity to reach a broad and diversified audience. By generating and distributing compelling content on social media, companies may attract new consumers and establish connections with current ones. Social media platforms also allow for customized advertising, which may help firms reach certain groups and increase the success of their marketing efforts.

To establish a successful social media marketing strategy, it's vital to first identify your objectives and target audience. From there, you may design a content plan that includes a mix of various forms of material, such as photographs, videos, blog entries, and infographics. It's also crucial to connect with your audience by replying to comments and messages and periodically providing fresh information.

When it comes to analyzing the performance of your social media marketing activities, there are numerous critical indicators to examine, including engagement rates, follower growth, website traffic, and conversions. By evaluating these analytics, you can alter your plan and increase the success of your social media marketing initiatives over time.

Social media marketing may be an efficient tool to enhance brand recognition, generate traffic and transactions, and develop lasting connections with consumers. Yet, it's crucial to approach social media marketing with a defined plan and a dedication to create interesting, high-quality content that connects with your target audience.

Search engine optimization (SEO)

Search engine optimization, usually known as SEO, is the activity of improving a website to maximize its exposure and ranking in search engine results pages (SERPs) (SERPs). The fundamental purpose of SEO is to increase organic visitors to a website by making it more visible to search engines like Google, Bing, and Yahoo.

There are numerous major components of SEO that are crucial for enhancing a website's ranking in search results. They include:

1. Keyword research - discovering the most relevant and high-traffic keywords that your target audience is looking for and implementing them into your website's content.

2. On-page optimization - improving the content and structure of your website, including title tags, meta descriptions, headers, and internal linking, to make it more visible and relevant to search engines.

3. Off-page SEO - generating high-quality backlinks from reliable websites to boost the authority and relevance of your website in the eyes of search engines.

4. Technical SEO - enhancing the technical characteristics of your website, including site speed, mobile-friendliness, and crawlability, to increase its overall performance and visibility in search results.

SEO needs continual work and a dedication to create high-quality, relevant content that connects with your target audience. By executing a thorough SEO plan, companies can enhance their visibility in search results, bring more visitors effectiveness of their campaigns in real-time, enabling them to make modifications to optimize their advertising for greater performance.

To establish a successful PPC advertising campaign, firms must undertake detailed keyword research and design attractive ad language and imagery that drives clicks. It's also crucial to ensure that landing pages are optimized for conversions, and to regularly evaluate and tweak campaigns for better outcomes.

Although PPC advertising may be an excellent approach to attract new consumers and improve revenue, it can also be pricey if not handled correctly. Marketers need to define clear targets, evaluate their expenditure and performance indicators, and adapt their campaigns as required to achieve a good return on investment (ROI) (ROI).

Email marketing

Email marketing is a sort of direct marketing that includes utilizing email to advertise a product or service, increase brand recognition, or nurture customer connections. It's a very efficient technique to contact your target audience and create a connection with them.

to their website, and eventually grow their online presence and reach.

It's vital to realize that SEO is a long-term process and may take time to see substantial benefits. Yet, the advantages of a well-executed SEO plan may be enormous, including greater search engine ranks, more website traffic, and a stronger online presence that can lead to higher conversions and income.

Pay per click (PPC) advertising

Pay per click (PPC) advertising is a digital advertising technique where marketers pay each time a user clicks on an ad. This sort of advertising may be seen on search engines, social media platforms, and other websites.

PPC advertising is often used to boost website traffic and sales by targeting certain keywords and demographics. Advertisers bid on relevant keywords and construct ad campaigns meant to draw clicks from prospective consumers.

One of the advantages of PPC advertising is that it can be highly targeted, enabling companies to reach particular demographics and enhance the success of their campaigns. Moreover, advertisers may analyze and assess the

Here are some pointers to help you make the most of your email marketing campaigns:

1. Create a quality email list: Your email list should be made up of individuals who have opted in to receive your emails, and who are interested in your goods or services. You may develop your email list by giving incentives like free downloads, exclusive content, or discounts.

2. Provide captivating content: Your email content should be interesting, useful, and relevant to your readers. You may add links to your blog articles, videos, or other stuff to keep your subscribers engaged and interested.

3. Customize your emails: Customization may assist enhance engagement and make your subscribers feel like they're receiving special attention. You may customize your emails by including the subscriber's name, segmenting your list, and employing relevant messages.

4. Employ a responsive design: More and more people are reading their emails on their mobile devices, therefore it's crucial you utilize a flexible design that adjusts to multiple screen sizes.

5. Test and optimize: Email marketing is a continually developing subject, so it's crucial to test and improve your efforts. You may experiment with alternative subject lines, send timings, and content to find what performs best with your audience.

6. Adopt best practices: Make sure your emails comply with anti-spam rules and give a simple mechanism for recipients to opt-out of your communications. You should also analyze your email deliverability and engagement rates to guarantee your promotions are successful.

Email marketing may be a great tool for creating connections with your audience and promoting your brand. By following these ideas, you can develop powerful email campaigns that engage and convert your readers.

Content marketing

Content marketing is a strategic approach to marketing that includes generating and delivering useful, relevant, and consistent information to attract and maintain a clearly defined audience and eventually generate lucrative consumer action. It is a long-term approach that focuses on creating connections with consumers via the development and distribution of excellent content.

One of the key purposes of content marketing is to promote the company or brand as a thought leader in its field by giving relevant information, insights, and answers to common issues that the target audience may be experiencing. This may be accomplished using a number of content kinds, including blog posts, videos, podcasts, e-books, infographics, white papers, and more.

To be successful, content marketing should be connected with the aims and values of the company or brand, and should be targeted to the requirements and interests of the target audience. This involves a comprehensive grasp of the audience's demographics, interests, pain points, and habits, as well as an awareness of how to successfully interact with them via the selected content kinds and channels.

One of the advantages of content marketing is that it may assist to increase organic traffic to a company or brand's website, as well as to social media platforms and other digital domains. This may lead to greater brand exposure, engagement, and eventually, conversions and sales. In addition, content marketing may assist to build the firm or brand as an expert in its sector, which can boost its reputation and credibility over time.

Chapter 3

Cybersecurity

Cybersecurity is a high-income talent that comprises a set of methods and procedures used to defend computer systems and networks against unauthorized access, data breaches, and other types of cyber assaults. Network security, ethical hacking, and data privacy are three fundamental issues within the discipline of cybersecurity that are extremely significant.

Network security covers the protection of computer networks against unauthorized access, hacking, and other cyber threats. It involves deploying security mechanisms like as firewalls, intrusion detection and prevention systems, and virtual private networks (VPNs) to prevent unwanted access and safeguard data in transit.

Ethical hacking, also known as penetration testing, involves detecting weaknesses in computer systems and networks by simulating assaults from possible hackers. Ethical hackers utilize the same tactics and tools as malevolent hackers, but with the objective of detecting and addressing security holes before they can be exploited.

Data privacy is concerned with ensuring the confidentiality, integrity, and availability of data. This involves installing encryption, access restrictions, and other steps to prevent unwanted access to sensitive data, as well as ensuring that data is not destroyed or damaged.

Workers with experience in network security, ethical hacking, and data privacy are in great demand in a broad variety of sectors, including banking, healthcare, and government. The demand for cybersecurity capabilities is driven by the increased danger of cyber assaults, which may result in considerable financial losses, harm to reputation, and legal liabilities.

Cybersecurity specialists may earn substantial wages, with many making six-figure salaries or more. The amount of competence necessary for various employment in the sector may vary, from entry-level positions in network security to more specialized ones in ethical hacking and data privacy.

It is a high-income skill with great career prospects and huge development potential. As the world grows more reliant on technology, the demand for cybersecurity specialists will only continue to expand.

Chapter 4

Blockchain and Cryptocurrency

Blockchain and cryptocurrency are currently expanding technologies that have opened up new options for companies, investors, and professionals. The blockchain is a decentralized digital ledger that records transactions in a safe and transparent way. Cryptocurrency, on the other hand, is a digital currency that functions on the blockchain and is utilized for financial transactions.

As these technologies continue to gain popularity, there is an increasing need for professionals who possess the knowledge and abilities essential to work with blockchain and cryptocurrencies. These talents may be very beneficial in a multitude of areas, from finance and banking to healthcare and logistics.

Workers that have knowledge in blockchain and cryptocurrencies may make significant incomes, especially in professions such as blockchain developers, cryptocurrency traders, and blockchain consultants. These candidates must possess a solid grasp of encryption, distributed systems, and programming languages such as Solidity and JavaScript.

Blockchain developers create and build decentralized apps (dApps) that are based on blockchain technology. They are responsible for establishing smart contracts, designing user interfaces, and implementing back-end infrastructure. According to Glassdoor, the average income for a blockchain engineer is $107,000 per year.

Cryptocurrency traders, on the other hand, purchase and sell digital currencies on exchanges. They must have a comprehensive awareness of market trends and be able to assess and interpret data in real-time. According to ZipRecruiter, the average compensation for a bitcoin trader is $102,828 per year.

Lastly, blockchain consultants give advice to corporations and organizations on how to implement blockchain technology into their operations. They must have a deep grasp of blockchain architecture and its applications, as well as expertise in project management and business development. According to ZipRecruiter, the average compensation for a blockchain consultant is $126,557 per year.

In summary, blockchain and cryptocurrency are quickly emerging sectors that provide a variety of high-income professional options. Professionals who have the knowledge and abilities to work with these technologies may earn great wages and find satisfying employment in a range of sectors.

Chapter 5
Artificial intelligence and machine learning

Artificial intelligence (AI) and machine learning (ML) are high in demand skills in the technology business. With the expanding usage of AI and ML in different businesses, the need for experts with knowledge in these areas is fast increasing. AI and ML specialists may specialize in numerous fields such as natural language processing (NLP), computer vision, and predictive modeling.

NLP is an area of AI that focuses on the interface between computers and human language. People that work in NLP employ algorithms and strategies to analyze, interpret, and produce natural language. They develop and construct chatbots, voice assistants, and other apps that engage with people using natural language. According to Glassdoor, the average income for an NLP engineer is $115,000 per year.

Computer vision is a branch of AI that deals with helping computers to recognize and interpret pictures and movies. Experts that work in computer vision employ ML algorithms to construct systems that can detect and categorize objects, people, and activities in photos and videos. They work in fields such as driverless cars, security systems, and medical imaging. According to Glassdoor, the typical income for a computer vision engineer is $130,000 per year.

Predictive modeling is a method used in ML to create predictions about future occurrences based on previous data. People that work in predictive modeling utilize statistical algorithms and ML approaches to construct models that can anticipate outcomes in fields such as finance, marketing, and healthcare. They deal with enormous data sets and employ methods such as regression analysis and decision trees. According to Glassdoor, the typical compensation for a predictive modeling analyst is $99,000 per year.

In conclusion, AI and ML specialists that specialize in NLP, computer vision, and predictive modeling are highly recognized in the market. They work on cutting-edge technologies that have a substantial influence on numerous sectors. The need for such specialists is projected to expand in the next few years, and they can expect to earn high wages while conducting tough and gratifying work.

Chapter 6
Cloud computing

Cloud computing is a fast emerging industry that is transforming the way companies and organizations work. It enables the development, administration, and storage of data and applications in a virtual environment, making it simpler for enterprises to access their information from anywhere in the globe. Cloud computing includes multiple components, including cloud infrastructure, security, and scalability.

Cloud infrastructure refers to the hardware and software components that make up a cloud computing system. It contains servers, storage devices, network devices, and other components that are utilized to build a virtual environment. Cloud infrastructure providers such as Amazon Web Services, Microsoft Azure, and Google Cloud Platform provide infrastructure-as-a-service (IaaS) solutions that enable organizations to rent the required infrastructure to operate their apps and store their data.

Security is a fundamental component of cloud computing. When data is kept in a virtual environment, it might be subject to security concerns. Cloud providers provide security features such as firewalls, encryption, and access control to guarantee that data is secured from unwanted access. Nevertheless, it is also the duty of the firm employing the cloud services to establish security best practices and guarantee that their data is appropriately safeguarded.

Scalability is another key component of cloud computing. Cloud infrastructure may be readily scaled up or down, depending on the requirements of the enterprise. This lets firms swiftly adapt their processing capacity to match variations in demand, such as spikes in traffic or seasonal oscillations. Scalability is particularly critical for firms that have unexpected or frequently changing workloads.

In summary, cloud computing has become a vital component of contemporary company operations. Cloud infrastructure, security, and scalability are critical components that allow enterprises to store and manage their data and applications in a virtual environment. Although the talent necessary to work in cloud computing may provide the opportunity for great pay, the value of cloud computing extends well beyond individual financial benefit.

Chapter 7

E-commerce

E-commerce is the buying and selling of products or services using the internet. It has been more popular in recent years, with more and more people flocking to online shopping for convenience, variety, and better offers. As a consequence, e-commerce has evolved as a high-income talent, with numerous chances for people to create their own online enterprises, operate as freelancers or consultants, or work for e-commerce organizations.

One of the most significant parts of e-commerce is online shop design. A well-designed e-commerce website can attract and keep consumers, make it simple for them to browse and buy items, and create a smooth shopping experience. Online shop design entails establishing a visually beautiful and user-friendly website that is optimized for search engines and mobile devices. This involves expertise of site design, user experience, and search engine optimization (SEO) (SEO).

Product sourcing is another key part of e-commerce. It entails choosing the correct things to market, negotiating with suppliers, and maintaining inventories. Product sourcing includes research and analysis to detect market trends and customer demand. Effective e-commerce enterprises also need to ensure that they obtain items at competitive pricing, so that they can give excellent value to their clients.

Customer service is a critical component of e-commerce, since it plays a significant role in creating and sustaining client loyalty. This comprises responding to client enquiries and concerns, offering help throughout the purchase process, and following up after the sale. Good customer service demands excellent communication and problem-solving abilities, as well as a dedication to satisfying client requirements.

Lastly, order fulfillment is the process of receiving and processing orders, choosing and packaging items, and sending them to clients. This demands attention to detail and good organizational abilities to guarantee that orders are delivered properly and effectively. Effective e-commerce enterprises need to have dependable and efficient order fulfillment systems in place to guarantee that consumers get their products in a timely way.

Overall, e-commerce provides numerous potential for people to build high-income talents in online shop design, product sourcing, customer care, and order fulfillment. With the correct information, abilities, and mentality, anybody can start a successful e-commerce firm or operate in the e-commerce sector.

Chapter 8

Mobile app development

Mobile app development has risen as a high-income talent in recent years, with the rising use of smartphones and mobile devices. Mobile app developers are in great demand and may make a considerable salary by designing unique and entertaining mobile applications for companies and people.

There are two primary mobile operating systems, iOS and Android, which have differing development needs. iOS app creation involves knowledge of Apple's programming language, Swift, and the development environment, Xcode. Android app development, on the other hand, needs knowledge of Java or Kotlin, and the Android Studio development environment.

In addition to programming languages, user experience (UX) and interface (UI) design are vital abilities for mobile app development. UX design entails understanding the demands and habits of people and building a simple and easy-to-use app interface. UI design entails producing the visual aspects and layout of the program, such as buttons, menus, and icons. Both UX and UI design need an eye for detail and a good grasp of human psychology.

Mobile app developers also need to be knowledgeable in several programming languages and frameworks, such as

JavaScript, React Native, and Node.js. They should also have a thorough grasp of data structures and algorithms, and be able to deal with APIs (Application Programming Interfaces) to interact with third-party services and platforms.

In addition to technical talents, mobile app developers also require excellent problem-solving and communication skills. They need to be able to grasp and interpret customer needs, interact with designers and other developers, and handle technological challenges.

Overall, mobile app development is a high-income talent that demands a mix of technical and interpersonal abilities. With the correct skills and expertise, mobile app developers may make a considerable salary by designing unique and entertaining mobile applications for companies and people.

Chapter 9

Video production

Video production is a profitable high-income skill that covers several areas, including video scripting, filming, editing, and distribution. Here's a summary of each of these characteristics and their importance in video production:

1. Video Scripting: This entails producing a screenplay that describes the content and message of the video. A strong screenplay is the cornerstone of every successful video production, since it serves to direct the shooting and editing procedures. A professional video screenwriter can build intriguing narratives, make convincing speeches, and design engaging tales that appeal with the audience.
2. Filming: Filming entails obtaining high-quality video footage using cameras and other equipment. A professional videographer knows lighting, composition, and camera angles, and can make aesthetically attractive movies that catch the attention of the audience.
3. Editing: After the material has been collected, a trained video editor takes over to convert it into a polished finished product. This entails trimming and rearranging film, adding special effects and transitions, and matching audio with images. A good video editor

can increase the quality of the film and produce a cohesive end product that interests the viewer.
4. Distribution: Lastly, video distribution entails bringing the finished product to the correct audience via social media, streaming services, or other channels. An experienced video marketer knows how to reach the target audience and optimize videos for maximum interaction and visibility.

Overall, video producing is a high-income trade that demands a mix of technical abilities and artistic creativity. A talented video producer who can manage all parts of video creation might earn a high salary by working for corporations, customers, or developing their own material for monetization. Also, with the rising demand for video content, there is a growing need for talented video producers, making it an appealing career path with great potential.

Chapter 10
Coaching and consulting

Coaching and consulting are highly regarded competencies that entail offering professional advice to people and businesses in numerous domains. These sectors are in great demand as people and corporations attempt to accomplish their objectives and overcome problems, making them a profitable alternative for those who have the skills and experience to give such advice.

If you're interested in developing a coaching or consulting firm, here are some recommendations to help you get started:

Identify your area of expertise: Pick a specialization or area of expertise that you are enthusiastic about and that corresponds with your abilities and experience. This can assist you deliver specialized, high-quality services and attract customers who are seeking your unique expertise.

Improve your skills: Constantly invest in your education and professional development to keep up-to-date with industry trends and changes. Attend classes, attend seminars, read books, and seek out mentoring to consistently develop your abilities and expertise.

Develop a business plan: Create a detailed business plan that details your company objectives, target market, services, pricing, and marketing tactics. This will help you keep focused and on track while you establish your coaching or consulting firm.

Develop your network: Establish contacts with prospective clients, industry experts, and other professionals who may recommend clients to you. Attend business conferences, networking events, and webinars to extend your network and develop your reputation.

Handle your clients: Establish clear expectations with your clients, create limits, and keep open communication. Build a system to handle customer queries, appointments, and follow-up interactions. Offering outstanding customer service can help you establish a loyal client base and attract new business.

Promote your services: Create a thorough marketing strategy that includes a website, social media presence, and content marketing. Utilize online channels such as LinkedIn and Instagram to display your skills and offer relevant material with your audience. Consider investing in paid advertising to reach a broader audience and generate traffic to your website.

Concentrate on providing outcomes: Your reputation as a coach or consultant will be founded on the results you produce. Concentrate on giving outstanding value to your customers, and ensuring that your services are personalized to match their individual requirements.

In conclusion, coaching and consulting are high-income talents that need a mix of experience, client management, and marketing ability to develop a successful firm. By following these recommendations and concentrating on offering outstanding value to your customers, you can establish yourself as a trusted adviser and develop a flourishing coaching or consulting firm.

Chapter 11

Product management

Project management is a fundamental skill that plays a significant part in helping businesses accomplish their goals and objectives. In today's corporate environment, project management is a highly sought-after ability and a high-income skill that may lead to rich employment prospects.

Project management is the process of planning, coordinating, and executing a project from start to completion. It involves a range of abilities, including leadership, communication, time management, problem-solving, and risk management, among others. These abilities assist project managers to guarantee that projects are completed within the assigned budget, time, and scope while achieving the quality criteria.

The need for project management skills has risen in recent years owing to the complicated and changing corporate environment. Businesses need professional project managers to handle their projects successfully and efficiently, which involves a high degree of knowledge and ability. Project managers are responsible for ensuring that projects are finished on schedule and within budget, which is vital to the success of any firm.

In addition, project management is a high-income skill that may lead to rich job prospects. According to the Project Management Institute (PMI), the typical income for a project manager in the United States is roughly $116,000 per year. This income might grow dependent on the degree of experience, education, and certification. In addition, project managers may work in a broad variety of sectors, including construction, information technology, healthcare, and finance, among others, which gives even more chances for development and progress.

To become a good project manager and make a large salary, one needs to gain the essential abilities and expertise. One may develop project management abilities via education, training, and certification programs. Organizations like PMI, Scrum Alliance, and Agile Alliance provide certification programs that give project managers the information and skills they need to thrive in their professions.

In conclusion, project management is a high-income talent that may lead to profitable employment prospects. It demands a particular set of skills and knowledge that may be gained via education, training, and certification programs. As the corporate environment gets more complicated and dynamic, the need for project management abilities is projected to continue to climb, making it a vital talent for people pursuing a high-income profession.

Chapter 12
Sales and negotiation

Sales and negotiating are very valued skills in today's corporate environment, and people who possess these skills have the opportunity to make a large salary. In this answer, I will explain prospecting, objection management, and closing strategies as critical components of effective sales and negotiation.

Prospecting is the process of locating prospective consumers and qualifying them as leads. It is a vital phase in the sales process as it helps salespeople to concentrate their efforts on individuals or organizations who are most likely to acquire their goods or services. Successful prospecting entails employing multiple tactics including networking, referrals, and web research to locate possible prospects. After leads have been found, salespeople need to qualify them by analyzing their requirements and determining if they are a suitable match for the product or service being provided.

Objection management is the skill of resolving and overcoming customer objections. It is typical for consumers to have reservations, fears, or questions about a product or service, and a successful salesman must be able to address these objections and give appealing answers. The key to good objection management is to listen actively to the customer, sympathize with their worries, then react with compelling reasons that answer their individual issues.

Closing strategies are the approaches used to convince a consumer to make a purchase. This is the last phase in the sales process, and it is crucial to employ efficient closing strategies to complete the purchase. The greatest closing strategies entail establishing a feeling of urgency, giving incentives or bonuses, and using persuasive language to convince the consumer to take action. It is crucial to be confident and forceful while employing closing strategies, but also to be respectful of the customer's choice.

In summary, sales and negotiating are high-income talents that demand proficiency in prospecting, objection management, and closing strategies. By mastering these abilities, sales professionals may effectively discover and qualify new leads, answer customer concerns, and convince clients to make a purchase. These abilities require time and experience to perfect, but with commitment and hard effort, anybody can become a good seller and negotiator.

Chapter 13
Data analysis and visualization

Data analysis and visualization are high income skills that are in great demand in today's work environment. In this answer, I will address data cleansing, statistical analysis, and data visualization approaches as critical components of effective data analysis and visualization.

Data cleaning is the process of discovering and resolving flaws, inconsistencies, and inaccuracies in data collections. It is a vital phase in the data analysis process, since the quality and dependability of insights and judgments derived from data rely on clean and correct data. Efficient data cleaning entails applying multiple tactics such as finding missing or wrong information, deleting duplicates, and addressing anomalies in data. After the data has been cleaned, it may be converted and readied for analysis.

Statistical analysis is the process of evaluating and analyzing data to uncover patterns, trends, and correlations between variables. It entails applying mathematical and statistical models to extract insights and create data-driven choices. Good statistical analysis requires choosing the proper statistical approach depending on the research topic, understanding the assumptions of the model, and interpreting the findings. Some typical statistical procedures include regression analysis, hypothesis testing, and correlation analysis.

Data visualization is the process of employing graphs, charts, and other visual aids to display data in a relevant and intelligent manner. Successful data visualization entails picking the proper visualization approach depending on the kind of data being studied, knowing the audience, and selecting the most effective manner to convey the results. Some typical visualization approaches include bar charts, line graphs, scatter plots, and heat maps.

In summary, data analysis and visualization are high-income talents that involve knowledge in data cleansing, statistical analysis, and data visualization approaches. By learning these abilities, data analysts and visualization specialists may effectively spot patterns and trends in data, extract insights, and make data-driven choices. These talents require time and effort to master, but with commitment and hard work, anybody can become a great data analyst or visualization specialist.

www.ingramcontent.com/pod-product-compliance
Lightning Source LLC
Chambersburg PA
CBHW071146220526
45467CB00015B/1991